MEDITERRANEAN

Refresh Cookbook

1200 Days of Easy, Tasty and Healthy Mouth-Watering Mediterranean Recipes for Beginners to living and Eating Well Every Day

Emma Allender

Warning-Disclaimer

The purpose of this book is to educate and entertain. The author or publisher does not guarantee that anyone following the techniques, suggestions, tips, ideas, or strategies will become successful. The author and publisher shall have neither liability or responsibility to anyone with respect to any loss or damage caused, or alleged to be caused, directly or indirectly by the information contained in this book.

Table of Content

INTRODUCTION

Welcome to the Mediterranean Diet world! This cookbook will introduce you to delicious and healthy Mediterranean cuisine. The Mediterranean Diet is more than a diet. It's a way to live that people have been enjoying for hundreds of years. This diet is based on the traditional eating habits of people in countries like Spain, Italy, Greece, and Morocco. It emphasizes fresh fruits and vegetables, lean proteins, and healthy oils.

Study suggests the Mediterranean Diet may be healthy. This includes a lower risk of developing heart disease and type 2 diabetes. It has been shown to improve brain function and increase lifespan. The Mediterranean Diet isn't a strict or trendy diet. It is a sustainable, enjoyable, and long-lasting way to eat that can be sustained over time.

This cookbook features a wide range of Mediterranean Diet recipes. These pages include delicious main dishes, hearty soups, and fresh salads. These recipes will inspire, no matter your level of experience with the Mediterranean Diet, to discover new ways to eat and reap the health benefits.

Grab a copy of the cookbook now and start exploring the healthy and delicious Mediterranean Diet!

The Science behind the Mediterranean Diet

The Mediterranean diet is a dietary pattern traditionally followed by people living in Mediterranean countries such as Greece, Italy, and Spain. Whole grains, legumes, Fruits, vegetables, nuts, and seeds take center stage, with fish, dairy, and chicken making up a small percentage of the diet. It also includes limited amounts of red meat, sweets, and processed foods.

There is a substantial body of scientific evidence that supports the health benefits of following a Mediterranean-style diet. Here are some of the key findings:

1. Reduced risk of cardiovascular disease: The Mediterranean diet has been linked in several studies to a decreased risk of cardiovascular disease. This may be due in part to the diet's emphasis on consuming healthy fats such as olive oil and nuts, as well as its high fiber content from whole grains and vegetables.
2. Improved cognitive function: Some research suggests that following a Mediterranean-style diet may help to improve cognitive function, including memory and attention. This may be due in part to the diet's anti-inflammatory effects, as well as its high levels of antioxidants and other beneficial nutrients.
3. Lower risk of certain cancers: Studies have found that following a Mediterranean-style diet is associated with a reduced risk of certain types of cancer, including breast cancer and colorectal cancer. This may be due in part to the diet's high levels of fiber, antioxidants, and other beneficial compounds.
4. Reduced inflammation: Studies have found that those who follow a Mediterranean diet have a lower chance of developing chronic illnesses like diabetes and arthritis.
5. Improved gut health: Some research suggests that the Mediterranean diet may help to promote the growth of beneficial gut bacteria, which can have a range of health benefits.

Overall, scientific evidence suggests that following a Mediterranean-style diet can have numerous health benefits. But, it's important to realize that a balanced diet is just one aspect of a healthy lifestyle, and other variables such as regular physical activity, stress management, and avoiding smoking are all vital for keeping good health.

What is the Mediterranean diet

The Mediterranean diet emphasizes the consumption of fruits, vegetables, legumes, seeds, whole grains, olive oil, and nuts. Red meat is a lesser part of the Mediterranean diet. Fish and seafood are important parts of it. Moderation is recommended for dairy products such as yogurt and cheese. To flavor food, herbs, and spices can be used instead of salt.

The Mediterranean diet encourages whole, minimally processed food consumption and discourages high-processed foods, added sugars, and saturated and trans fats.

The Mediterranean diet is a sustainable and healthy way to eat that promotes good health and helps prevent chronic diseases.

Health Benefits of the Mediterranean Diet

The Mediterranean diet is primarily based on healthy plant foods, including fresh fruits and vegetables. It also includes daily activities such as walking, biking, and olive oil. This diet helps reduce your risk of many diseases and keeps you healthy and fit. These are just a few of the many health benefits that diet can bring to your body.

Heart health is improved: The Mediterranean diet does not allow for high-processed and refined foods. The Mediterranean diet focuses on eating a lot of monounsaturated fats and omega-3 to increase HDL (good cholesterol) and decrease LDL (bad cholesterol). It can improve your heart health and reduce the risk of heart diseases such as stroke and heart attack.

Protects against type-2 diabetes: The Mediterranean diet is high in fiber and low in carbohydrates. It also contains high levels of protein. It controls the hormones that regulate insulin and blood sugar levels, which helps prevent type-2 diabetes. Fiber-rich diets slow down the digestion process and prevent blood sugar spikes.

Increase your lifespan: Mediterranean foods are rich in nutrients, minerals, and vitamins. High levels of antioxidants help to reduce cell damage and oxidative stress. Anti-inflammatory properties in Mediterranean foods can help reduce depression and improve mood. Monounsaturated fats are a major component of the Mediterranean diet, which includes olive oil. Monounsaturated fats can reduce your risk of developing heart disease, cancer, or inflammatory diseases and increase your life expectancy.

Combat depression with the Mediterranean diet. It has anti-inflammatory properties. This will reduce your depression and improve your mood. Research shows that people who eat the Mediterranean diet have a lower risk of developing depression by 98 percent. Reduce your risk of cancer: Studies and research on the Mediterranean diet have shown that it can increase your immunity to combat cancers like breast cancer, colon cancer, and uterine carcinoma. It reduces the risk of dying from cancer.

CHAPTER 2: BREAKFAST

Eggs with Spinach & Chard

Serving: 4

Preparation time: 10 minutes

Cooking time: 15 minutes

Ingredients:

- 2 cups of fresh spinach, washed and chopped
- 2 cups of fresh Swiss chard, washed and chopped
- 1 tbsp olive oil
- 1 small onion, chopped
- 2 garlic cloves, minced
- 4 eggs
- Salt and pepper to taste

Instructions:

1. Melt the olive oil in a large pan over medium heat.
2. Cook the chopped onion for approximately 5 minutes, or until it starts to turn translucent.
3. After one more minute, add the minced garlic.
4. Sliced spinach and chard should be added to the skillet and cooked for 2-3 minutes, turning periodically, until wilted.
5. The spinach and chard mixture should be divided into 4 wells. Crack an egg into each well.
6. Season the eggs with salt and pepper to taste.
7. Cover the skillet and cook until the egg whites are set and the yolks are still runny about 5-7 minutes.
8. Serve hot.

Cinnamon Almond Quinoa

Serving: 4

Preparation time: 5 minutes

Cooking time: 20 minutes

Ingredients:

- 1 cup of quinoa, rinsed and drained
- 2 cups of water
- 1/2 tsp ground cinnamon
- 1/4 tsp ground nutmeg
- 1/4 tsp salt
- 1/4 cup of chopped almonds
- 1 tbsp honey
- 1/4 cup of milk (almond milk or dairy milk)
- Optional toppings: fresh berries, chopped apples, additional chopped nuts, and honey

Instructions:

1. In a medium saucepan, combine the quinoa, water, cinnamon, nutmeg, and salt. Bring to a boil over high heat.
2. Reduced the heat to low, cover the saucepan, and simmer for 16-20 minutes or until the water is absorbed and the quinoa is soft.
3. Remove the saucepan from the heat and fluff the quinoa with a fork.
4. Stir in the chopped almonds, honey, and milk.
5. Serve hot or chilled with optional toppings, if desired.

Spinach Pepper Olive Egg Muffins

Serving: 12 egg muffins

Preparation time: 10 minutes

Cooking time: 20-25 minutes

Ingredients

- 8 eggs
- 1/4 cup of milk
- 1/4 tsp salt
- 1/4 tsp black pepper
- 1/2 cup of chopped spinach
- 1/2 cup of chopped red bell pepper
- 1/4 cup of chopped kalamata olives
- Cooking spray

Instructions

1. Preheat the oven to 350°F. Grease a 12-cup of a muffin tin with cooking spray.
2. In a mixing bowl, mix together the eggs, milk, salt, and pepper.
3. Add the chopped spinach, red bell pepper, and kalamata olives to the egg mixture and stir to combine.
4. Divide the egg mixture evenly among the 12 muffin cups.
5. Bake in the preheated oven for 22-25 minutes or until the egg muffins are set, and the edges are lightly browned.
6. Take the muffins from the oven and let them cool for a few minutes before removing them from the muffin tin.
7. Serve warm or cold.

Tomato Spinach Frittata

Serving: 6

Preparation time: 10 minutes

Cooking time: 25-30 minutes

Ingredients

- 8 eggs
- 1/4 cup of milk
- 1/4 tsp salt
- 1/4 tsp black pepper
- 1 cup of cherry tomatoes, halved
- 2 cups of fresh spinach leaves
- 1/2 cup of shredded cheddar cheese
- 1 tbsp olive oil

Instructions

1. Set the oven's temperature to 375°F (190°C).
2. Mix the eggs, milk, salt, and pepper in a mixing dish.
3. In a 10-inch oven-safe skillet, heat the olive oil over medium heat.
4. The cherry tomatoes should start to soften after being added to the skillet and cooked for two to three minutes.
5. Fresh spinach leaves should be added to the skillet and cooked for 1-2 minutes, or until wilted.
6. Over the sautéed veggies in the skillet, pour the egg mixture.
7. Over the egg mixture, top with the crumbled cheddar cheese.
8. The frittata should be cooked on the stovetop for 3 to 4 minutes, or until the edges begin to firm.
9. After the frittata has set and the top is golden, place the pan in the preheated oven and bake for 15-20 minutes.
10. Before slicing and serving, take the pan out of the oven and let it to cool for a while.

Veggie Quinoa Egg Muffins

Serving: 12 egg muffins

Preparation time: 10 minutes

Cooking time: 20-25 minutes

Ingredients

- 6 eggs
- 1/4 cup of milk
- 1/4 tsp salt
- 1/4 tsp black pepper
- 1 cup of cooked quinoa
- 1/2 cup of chopped spinach
- 1/2 cup of chopped red bell pepper
- 1/4 cup of shredded cheddar cheese
- Cooking spray

Instructions

1. Preheat the oven to 375°F. Grease a 12-cup of a muffin tin with cooking spray.
2. In a mixing bowl, mix together the eggs, milk, salt, and pepper.
3. Add the cooked quinoa, chopped spinach, and chopped red bell pepper to the egg mixture and stir to combine.
4. Divide the egg mixture evenly among the 12 muffin cups.
5. Sprinkle the shredded cheddar cheese over the top of the egg mixture in each muffin cup.
6. Bake in the preheated oven for 22-25 minutes or until the egg muffins are set, and the edges are lightly browned.
7. Take the muffins from the oven and let them cool for a few minutes before removing them from the muffin tin.
8. Serve warm or cold.

Greek Breakfast Omelet

Serving: 1

Preparation time: 5 minutes

Cooking time: 10 minutes

Ingredients:

- 3 eggs
- 1 tbsp water
- 1/4 tsp salt
- 1/4 tsp black pepper
- 1/4 cup of crumbled feta cheese
- 1/4 cup of chopped Kalamata olives
- 1/4 cup of chopped tomatoes
- 1/4 cup of chopped fresh spinach
- 1 tbsp olive oil

Instructions:

1. In a mixing bowl, mix together the eggs, water, salt, and pepper.
2. Heat the olive oil in a non-stick skillet over medium heat.
3. Add the chopped tomatoes to the skillet and cook for 2-3 minutes or until they start to soften.
4. Add the chopped fresh spinach to the skillet and cook for 1-2 minutes or until it is wilted.
5. Pour the egg mixture into the skillet over the cooked vegetables.
6. Sprinkle the crumbled feta cheese and chopped Kalamata olives over one-half of the omelet.
7. Used a spatula to fold the other half of the omelet over the filling.
8. Cooked for an additional 2 minutes or until the egg is set and the cheese is melted.
9. Slide the omelet onto a plate and serve.

Spinach Egg Scramble

Serving: 1

Preparation time: 5 minutes

Cooking time: 5 minutes

Ingredients:

- 2 eggs
- 1/4 tsp salt
- 1/4 tsp black pepper
- 1/2 cup of fresh spinach leaves, chopped
- 1 tbsp butter or olive oil

Instructions:

1. In a mixing bowl, mix together the eggs, salt, and pepper.
2. Heat the butter or olive oil in a non-stick skillet over medium heat.
3. Add the chopped fresh spinach to the skillet and cook for 1-2 minutes or until it is wilted.
4. Pour the egg mixture into the skillet over the cooked spinach.
5. Using a spatula to scramble the eggs and spinach together until the eggs are fully cooked and no longer runny.
6. Remove from heat and serve.

Quinoa Mushroom Muffins

Serving: 12 muffins

Preparation time: 15 minutes

Cooking time: 25-30 minutes

Ingredients

- 1 cup of cooked quinoa
- 1/2 cup of chopped mushrooms
- 1/2 cup of chopped onion
- 1/4 cup of chopped fresh parsley
- 1/4 cup of grated Parmesan cheese
- 1/4 cup of all-purpose flour
- 2 eggs
- 1 tsp baking powder
- 1/2 tsp salt
- 1/4 tsp black pepper
- Cooking spray

Instructions

1. Preheat the oven to 350°F. Grease a 12-cup of a muffin tin with cooking spray.
2. In a mixing bowl, combine the cooked quinoa, chopped mushrooms, chopped onion, chopped fresh parsley, grated Parmesan cheese, all-purpose flour, eggs, baking powder, salt, and black pepper.
3. Stir the mixture until everything is evenly combined.
4. Spoon the mixture into the prepared muffin tin, filling each cup about 3/4 full.
5. The muffins should be golden brown and a toothpick put into the center should come out clean after 25–30 minutes in the preheated oven.
6. Take the muffins from the oven and allow them cool in the muffin pan.
7. Serve cold or hot.

Broccoli Cheese Egg Bake

Serving: 4

Preparation time: 10 minutes

Cooking time: 25-30 minutes

Ingredients

- 6 eggs
- 1/2 cup of milk
- 1/2 tsp salt
- 1/4 tsp black pepper
- 1/2 tsp garlic powder
- 2 cups of chopped broccoli florets
- 1 cup of shredded cheddar cheese
- 1 tbsp olive oil

Instructions

1. Preheat the oven to 375°F. Grease a 9-inch baking dish with olive oil.
2. In a mixing bowl, mix together the eggs, milk, salt, black pepper, and garlic powder.
3. Stir in the chopped broccoli florets and shredded cheddar cheese.
4. Pour the mixture into the prepared baking dish.
5. Bake in the preheated oven for 28-30 minutes or until the egg is set and the cheese is melted and golden brown.
6. Removed from the oven and let it cool for a some minutes before slicing and serving.

Almond Oatmeal

Serving: 2

Preparation time: 2 minutes

Cooking time: 7 minutes

Ingredients

- 1 cup of rolled oats
- 2 cups of water
- 1/2 cup of almond milk
- 1/4 cup of chopped almonds
- 1/4 tsp salt
- 1/2 tsp cinnamon
- 1 tbsp honey or maple syrup (optional)

Instructions

1. In a medium saucepan, combine the rolled oats, water, almond milk, chopped almonds, salt, and cinnamon.
2. Bring the mixture to a boil over medium-high heat.
3. Reduced the heat to low and simmer for 5-7 minutes or until the oats are cooked, and the mixture has thickened.
4. Removed from the heat and let it cool for a few minutes.
5. If desired, stir in the honey or maple syrup for added sweetness.
6. Serve warm.

Spinach Leek Egg Muffins

Serving: 12 muffins

Preparation time: 10 minutes

Cooking time: 20-25 minutes

Ingredients

- 6 eggs
- 1/4 cup of milk
- 1/4 tsp salt
- 1/4 tsp black pepper
- 1 cup of chopped fresh spinach
- 1/2 cup of chopped leeks
- 1/2 cup of shredded cheddar cheese
- Cooking spray

Instructions

1. Preheat the oven to 350°F. Grease a 12-cup of a muffin tin with cooking spray.
2. In a mixing bowl, mix together the eggs, milk, salt, and black pepper.
3. Stir in the chopped spinach, chopped leeks, and shredded cheddar cheese.
4. Spoon the mixture into the prepared muffin tin, filling each cup about 3/4 full.
5. Bake for 20 to 25 minutes in a preheated oven, or until golden brown and a toothpick inserted in the center of a muffin comes out clean.
6. The muffins should be taken out of the oven and allowed to cool in the pan for a few minutes before being removed.
7. Cold or warm serving.

Mix Veggie Egg Muffins

Serving: 12 muffins

Preparation time: 15 minutes

Cooking time: 20-25 minutes

Ingredients:

- 6 eggs
- 1/4 cup of milk
- 1/4 tsp salt
- 1/4 tsp black pepper
- 1/2 cup of chopped red bell pepper
- 1/2 cup of chopped green bell pepper
- 1/2 cup of chopped onion
- 1/2 cup of chopped zucchini
- 1/2 cup of shredded cheddar cheese
- Cooking spray

Instructions:

1. Preheat the oven to 350°F. Grease a 12-cup of a muffin tin with cooking spray.
2. In a mixing bowl, mix together the eggs, milk, salt, and black pepper.
3. Stir in the chopped red bell pepper, chopped green bell pepper, chopped onion, chopped zucchini, and shredded cheddar cheese.
4. Spoon the mixture into the prepared muffin tin, filling each cup about 3/4 full.
5. The muffins should be golden brown and a toothpick put into the center should come out clean after 20–25 minutes in the preheated oven.
6. Take the muffins from the oven and allow them cool in the muffin pan.
7. Serve cold or hot.

Simple Breakfast Quiche

Serving: 6

Preparation time: 10 minutes

Cooking time: 35-40 minutes

Ingredients

- 1 pre-made pie crust
- 6 eggs
- 1/2 cup of milk
- 1/2 tsp salt
- 1/4 tsp black pepper
- 1/2 cup of chopped cooked bacon or ham
- 1/2 cup of shredded cheddar cheese
- 1/4 cup of chopped green onions

Instructions

1. Preheat the oven to 375°F. Place the pre-made pie crust in a 9-inch pie dish.
2. In a mixing bowl, whisk together the eggs, milk, salt, and black pepper.
3. Stir in the chopped cooked bacon or ham, shredded cheddar cheese, and chopped green onions.
4. Pour the mixture into the prepared pie crust.
5. Bake in the preheated oven for 38-40 minute.
6. Take the quiche from the oven and let it cool for a some minutes before slicing and serving.
7. Serve warm or at room temperature.

Spicy Egg Bake

Serving: 4-6

Preparation time: 10 minutes

Cooking time: 25-30 minutes

Ingredients

- 8 eggs
- 1/2 cup of milk
- 1/2 tsp salt
- 1/4 tsp black pepper
- 1/4 tsp cayenne pepper
- 1/2 cup of cooked and crumbled sausage
- 1/2 cup of chopped bell peppers
- 1/2 cup of shredded cheddar cheese
- Cooking spray

Instructions

1. Preheat the oven to 350°F. Use cooking spray to grease a 9-inch baking pan.
2. Mix together the eggs, milk, and salt in a large bowl.
3. Mix in the cooked and crumbled sausages, chopped bell peppers and shredded cheddar cheese.
4. Put the mixture in the prepared baking dish.
5. Bake for 25-30 minutes in the oven or until the egg bake has set and the top is golden brown.
6. Let the egg bake cool in the oven for a few minutes before cutting and serving.
7. Warm or at room temperature.

Herb Egg Muffins

Serving: 6

Preparation time: 10 minutes

Cooking time: 20-25 minutes

Ingredients

- 8 eggs
- 1/2 cup of milk
- 1/2 tsp salt
- 1/4 tsp black pepper
- 1/4 cup of chopped fresh herbs
- 1/2 cup of shredded cheddar cheese
- Cooking spray

Instructions:

1. Preheat oven to 375°F (190°C). Use cooking spray to grease a 12-cup muffin pan.
2. Mix the eggs, milk and salt in a large bowl.
3. Mix in the chopped fresh herbs and shredded cheddar cheese.
4. Place the mixture in a muffin pan.
5. Bake the muffins in the oven for 20-25 mins or until they are cooked through and the tops are golden brown.
6. Let the egg muffins cool in the oven for a few minutes, then remove them from the muffin pan.
7. Warm or at room temperature.

CHAPTER 3: LUNCH RECIPES

Delicious Chickpea in Skillet

Serving: 4

Preparation time: 10 minutes

Cooking time: 15 minutes

Ingredients

- 2 tbsp olive oil
- 1 small onion, diced
- 2 cloves garlic, minced
- 1 red bell pepper, diced
- 1 yellow bell pepper, diced
- 2 cans chickpeas, drained and rinsed
- 1 tsp cumin
- 1 tsp smoked paprika
- 1/2 tsp salt
- 1/4 tsp black pepper
- 1/4 cup of chopped fresh parsley
- 2 tbsp lemon juice

Instructions

1. Place the olive oil in an oven-proof skillet on medium heat.
2. Sauté the diced onion for 2 to 3 minutes or until it starts to soften.
3. Sauté the minced garlic, diced bell peppers and the remaining ingredients in the skillet for 3-4 minutes until the peppers become tender.
4. The drained chickpeas should be tossed in with the salt, black pepper, smoked paprika and cumin. Mix well.
5. The chickpea mixture should be cooked for about 5-7 minutes or until it is slightly browned and heated through.
6. Turn off the heat in the skillet and add the chopped fresh parsley, lemon juice and spices.
7. As a side dish, or as a main dish for vegetarians, you can serve the chickpea mixture over rice or quinoa.

Spinach Chickpea Quinoa

Serving: 4

Preparation time: 10 minutes

Cooking time: 25 minutes

Ingredients

- 1 cup of quinoa
- 2 cups of water
- 2 tbsp olive oil
- 1 small onion, diced
- 2 cloves garlic, minced
- 1 red bell pepper, diced
- 1 can chickpeas, drained and rinsed
- 2 cups of fresh spinach, chopped
- 1/2 tsp ground cumin
- 1/2 tsp ground coriander
- 1/4 tsp salt
- 1/4 tsp black pepper
- 1/4 cup of chopped fresh cilantro
- 2 tbsp lemon juice

Instructions

1. Rinse the Quinoa in a fine mesh strainer. Then, add 2 cups of water to a medium saucepan. Bring the mixture to a boil. Then reduce the heat to low, cover and let it cool. Let it simmer for about 15-20 minutes or until all the water has been absorbed and the Quinoa is tender.
2. Heat the olive oil in a large skillet on medium heat. Sauté the diced onion for 2 to 3 minutes or until it starts to soften.
3. Sauté the minced garlic, diced bell pepper, and the remaining ingredients in the skillet for 3-4 minutes until the peppers become tender.
4. Mix the chickpeas with the water in the skillet. Stir to combine.
5. Place the chopped spinach in a skillet. Cook for about 1-2 minutes or until the spinach is tender.
6. Mix in the ground cumin and ground coriander. Season with salt and black pepper.
7. Stir the cooked Quinoa into the skillet.
8. Stir in the lemon juice and chopped fresh cilantro.

9. Warm spinach chickpea quinoa can be served as a side or main dish for vegetarians.

Spicy Skillet Zucchini

Serving: 4

Preparation time: 10 minutes

Cooking time: 10 minutes

Ingredients

- 2 tbsp olive oil
- 2 medium zucchinis, sliced
- 1 small onion, sliced
- 2 cloves garlic, minced
- 1 tsp chili powder
- 1/2 tsp cumin
- 1/2 tsp paprika
- Salt and pepper to taste
- 1/4 cup of chopped fresh cilantro

Instructions

1. Place the olive oil in an oven-proof skillet on medium heat.
2. Sauté the onion and zucchini slices in a skillet for 3-4 minutes or until they soften.
3. Sauté the minced garlic in the skillet for one more minute.
4. Mix the cumin, chili powder, salt, paprika and pepper into the zucchini mixture. Stir well to combine.
5. Continue to cook for 2-3 minutes or until the zucchini is tender.
6. Stir in the chopped cilantro and remove the skillet from the heat.
7. The spicy skillet zucchini can be served as a side dish or as a main dish for vegetarians.

Healthy Zucchini Salad:

Serving: 4

Preparation time: 15 minutes

Cooking time: 0

Ingredients

- 2 medium zucchinis, sliced into thin rounds
- 1 small red onion, thinly sliced
- 1/2 cup of crumbled feta cheese
- 1/4 cup of chopped fresh parsley
- 2 tbsp extra-virgin olive oil
- 2 tbsp fresh lemon juice
- 1 clove garlic, minced
- Salt and pepper to taste

Instructions

1. Combine the chopped red onion, feta cheese crumbled, and zucchini sliced in a large bowl.
2. Mix the olive oil with lemon juice, minced garlic and salt in a small bowl.
3. Toss the mixture with the dressing.
4. Allow the salad to sit for about 10-15 minutes so that the flavors can meld.
5. You can serve the zucchini salad as a side dish, or you can add shrimp or grilled chicken to make it a full meal.

Quinoa Veggie Risotto

Serving: 4

Preparation time: 10 minutes

Cooking time: 30 minutes

Ingredients

- 1 cup of quinoa, rinsed and drained
- 2 tbsp olive oil
- 1 small onion, diced
- 2 cloves garlic, minced
- 1 medium zucchini, diced
- 1 red bell pepper, diced
- 4 cups of vegetable broth
- 1/4 cup of grated Parmesan cheese
- Salt and pepper to taste
- Fresh parsley or basil for garnish (optional)

Instructions

1. Heat the olive oil in a large saucepan on medium heat.
2. Sauté the minced garlic and diced onion in the pan until translucent, approximately 3-4 minutes.
3. Sauté the red bell pepper and diced zucchini in the pan for 3-4 minutes.
4. Mix the quinoa with the oil in a saucepan. Stir well.
5. Stir the vegetable broth into a pan. The mixture should be brought to a simmer. Cook for between 20 and 25 minutes, occasionally stirring until the quinoa becomes tender and the broth is absorbed.
6. Mix in the grated Parmesan cheese. Season with salt and pepper.
7. If desired, serve the quinoa vegetable risotto warm with fresh basil or parsley garnished.

Healthy Olive Couscous:

Serving: 4

Preparation time: 10 minutes

Cooking time: 15 minutes

Ingredients:

- 1 cup of couscous
- 1 1/4 cups of boiling water
- 2 tbsp olive oil
- 1 small onion, diced
- 2 cloves garlic, minced
- 1 red bell pepper, diced
- 1/2 cup of pitted kalamata olives, chopped
- 1/4 cup of chopped fresh parsley
- 2 tbsp fresh lemon juice
- Salt and pepper to taste

Instructions:

1. Pour the boiling water over the couscous. Then cover the bowl with plastic wrap or a lid and allow it to sit for 10 minutes so that the water absorbs.
2. Heat the olive oil in a large skillet on medium heat.
3. Sauté the minced garlic and diced onion in the skillet until translucent, approximately 3-4 minutes.
4. Sauté the diced red bell Pepper in the skillet for 3-4 minutes.
5. Stir the chopped Kalamata olives into the skillet.
6. Mix the couscous in a bowl with a fork. Add it to the skillet along with the vegetables and olives. Mix well.
7. Stir in the chopped parsley and fresh lemon juice and mix well.
8. Season the olive couscous to your liking with salt and pepper.
9. You can serve the olive couscous as a side dish or add grilled chicken or fish for a complete meal.

Sweet Lime Salmon

Serving: 4

Preparation time: 40 minutes

Cooking time: 12-15 minutes

Ingredients

- 4 salmon fillets
- 1/4 cup of fresh lime juice
- 2 tbsp honey
- 2 cloves garlic, minced
- 1 tsp ground cumin
- 1 tsp smoked paprika
- Salt and pepper to taste
- 1 tbsp olive oil
- Lime wedges for serving

Instructions

1. Mix together the honey, lime juice, honeycomb, minced garlic, and smoked paprika in a small bowl. Season with salt.
2. Place the salmon fillets on a plate and then pour the lime marinade over it. The marinade should be evenly coated on the salmon fillets using your hands. Allow the salmon to marinate for at least 30 minutes and up to 2 hours in the refrigerator.
3. Preheat your oven to 400°F (200°C).
4. Over medium heat, heat the olive oil in an oven-safe saucepan.
5. Place the salmon skin-side up in the skillet. The marinade should be kept aside.
6. The salmon can be cooked on the stovetop for 2 to 3 minutes, and then the skillet should go into the oven.
7. Bake the salmon for between 8-10 minutes, or until you are satisfied with its texture.
8. The salmon should be baking while the marinade is simmering in a small saucepan. Let the marinade simmer on medium heat for about 5-10 minutes, stirring every now and then, until it thickens and reduces by half.
9. After the salmon has been cooked, take it out of the oven and let it cool for a while.
10. Serve the salmon fillets with the reduced marinade drizzled over them.

Parmesan Salmon

Serving: 4

Preparation time: 10 minutes

Cooking time: 12-15 minutes

Ingredients

- 4 salmon fillets
- 1/4 cup of grated Parmesan cheese
- 1/4 cup of panko breadcrumbs
- 2 tbsp chopped fresh parsley
- 1 tbsp olive oil
- 1 tsp garlic powder
- Salt and pepper to taste
- Lemon wedges for serving

Instructions

1. Preheat your oven to 425°F (220°C). Place parchment paper on a baking sheet.
2. Combine the panko breadcrumbs, grated Parmesan cheese and chopped parsley in a small bowl. Season with olive oil, garlic powder salt, and pepper.
3. Place salmon fillets, skin side down, on the baking sheet.
4. Spread the Parmesan mixture evenly over each salmon fillet using your hands. Press gently to ensure it sticks.
5. Bake the salmon for between 12-15 minutes or until it is cooked through and the Parmesan crust turns golden brown and crispy.
6. After the salmon has been cooked, take it out of the oven and let it cool for a while.
7. Serve salmon fillets with lemon wedges.

Parmesan Pesto Tilapia

Serving: 4

Preparation time: 10 minutes

Cooking time: 12-15 minutes

Ingredients

- 4 tilapia fillets
- 1/4 cup of prepared basil pesto
- 1/4 cup of grated Parmesan cheese
- 1/4 cup of panko breadcrumbs
- 2 tbsp chopped fresh parsley
- Salt and pepper to taste
- Lemon wedges for serving

Instructions

1. Preheat your oven to 375°F (190°C). Place parchment paper on a baking sheet.
2. Combine the basil pesto with grated Parmesan cheese and panko breadcrumbs. Add chopped parsley, salt and pepper.
3. Place the tilapia fillets onto the baking sheet.
4. Spread the pesto mixture evenly over each tilapia fillet using your hands. Press gently to ensure it sticks.
5. Bake the tilapia in the oven for 12-15 minutes or until it is cooked through and the Parmesan crust turns golden brown and crispy.
6. After the tilapia has been cooked, take it out of the oven and let it cool for a while.
7. Serve the tilapia fillets alongside lemon wedges.

Shrimp Mushroom Stir Fry:

Serving: 4

Preparation time: 10 minutes

Cooking time: 15 minutes

Ingredients:

- 1 lb. large shrimp, peeled and deveined
- 8 oz. sliced mushrooms
- 1 red bell pepper, thinly sliced
- 1 green bell pepper, thinly sliced
- 1 small onion, thinly sliced
- 3 cloves garlic, minced
- 2 tbsp olive oil
- 2 tbsp soy sauce
- 1 tbsp oyster sauce
- 1 tbsp cornstarch
- Salt and pepper to taste
- Steamed rice for serving

Instructions:

1. Mix together the oyster sauce, soy sauce, cornstarch and 1/4 cup water in a small bowl. Set aside.
2. Over medium heat, heat the olive oil in large skillets or woks.
3. Sauté the garlic for about 30 seconds or until fragrant
4. In a skillet, add the red and green bell peppers, sliced mushrooms, and onion. Sauté for 3-4 minutes or until vegetables are lightly softened.
5. Sauté the shrimp in the skillet for 2-3 minutes or until they are opaque and pink.
6. Mix the soy sauce over the vegetables and shrimp. Stir to coat.
7. Continue cooking for 2-3 minutes or until sauce thickens and shrimp and vegetables are coated.
8. Salt and pepper to your liking
9. Serve the shrimp and mushroom stir-fry over steamed rice.

Lemon Herb Tilapia

Serving: 4

Preparation time: 10 minutes

Cooking time: 10-12 minutes

Ingredients

- 4 tilapia fillets
- 2 tbsp olive oil
- 2 tbsp lemon juice
- 2 tbsp fresh parsley, chopped
- 2 tbsp fresh basil, chopped
- 1 tsp dried oregano
- 1/2 tsp garlic powder
- Salt and pepper to taste
- Lemon wedges for serving

Instructions

1. Preheat the oven to 400°F (200°C).
2. Mix the olive oil, lemon zest, parsley, basil and garlic powder in a small bowl. Season with salt and pepper.
3. Place the tilapia fillets on a baking tray and spread the herb mixture evenly.
4. Bake for between 10-12 minutes or until the tilapia flakes easily when tapped with a fork.
5. Serve the lemon herb Tilapia hot with lemon wedges.

Lemon Garlic Scallops

Serving: 4

Preparation time: 10 minutes

Cooking time: 6-8 minutes

Ingredients

- 1 lb. fresh sea scallops, cleaned and patted dry
- 2 tbsp. butter
- 2 tbsp. olive oil
- 3 cloves garlic, minced
- 1 tbsp. lemon zest
- 2 tbsp. fresh lemon juice
- Salt and pepper, to taste
- 2 tbsp. fresh parsley, chopped

Instructions

1. Place a large skillet on medium heat.
2. Place the butter and olive oils in a skillet. Let the butter melt.
3. Place the scallops in a skillet. Cook for 2 to 3 minutes or until golden brown.
4. Cook the garlic in the skillet for 30 seconds or until fragrant
5. Stir the lemon zest, lemon juice and olive oil into the skillet.
6. Season the scallops with salt to taste.
7. Serve immediately with the chopped parsley sprinkled over the scallops.

Greek Cod

Serving: 4

Preparation time: 10 minutes

Cooking time: 15-20 minutes

Ingredients

- 4 cod fillets
- 2 tbsp. olive oil
- 2 garlic cloves, minced
- 1 tbsp. dried oregano
- 1 tsp. dried thyme
- 1 tsp. dried basil
- 1/2 tsp. salt
- 1/4 tsp. black pepper
- 1 lemon, sliced
- 1/4 cup of crumbled feta cheese
- 2 tbsp. chopped fresh parsley

Instructions

1. Turn the oven on to 375°F.
2. Olive oil, garlic, oregano, thyme, basil, salt, and black pepper should all be combined in a small bowl.
3. Cod fillets should be placed on a baking dish and should be brushed with the olive oil mixture.
4. Lemon slices are placed on top of each fillet.
5. Bake the fish for 15-20 minutes, or until it is well cooked and flakes with a fork.
6. The cod fillets should be topped with feta cheese crumbles and chopped parsley.
7. Serving hot, please.

Shrimp Skewers

Serving: 4

Preparation time: 15 minutes

Cooking time: 8-10 minutes

Ingredients

- 1 lb. large shrimp, peeled and deveined
- 1 red bell pepper, cut into 1-inch pieces
- 1 yellow bell pepper, cut into 1-inch pieces
- 1 zucchini, cut into 1/2-inch rounds
- 1 red onion, cut into 1-inch pieces
- 1/4 cup of olive oil
- 2 garlic cloves, minced
- 2 tbsp. lemon juice
- 1 tsp. dried oregano
- 1/2 tsp. salt
- 1/4 tsp. black pepper
- Wooden skewers, soaked in water for 30 minutes

Instructions

1. Mix the olive oil, garlic, lemon juice, oregano, salt, and black pepper in a large bowl.
2. Bell peppers, zucchini, red onion, and shrimp should all be added to the bowl and coated.
3. When you thread the ingredients onto the skewers, alternate the shrimp and veggies.
4. Grill or grill pan should be heated to medium-high.
5. For the shrimp to be pink and cooked through, grill the skewers for 3–4 minutes on each side.
6. Serving hot, please.

Balsamic Chicken

Serving: 4

Preparation time: 10 minutes

Cooking time: 25-30 minutes.

Ingredients

- 4 boneless, skinless chicken breasts
- 1/4 cup of balsamic vinegar
- 2 tbsp. olive oil
- 2 tbsp. honey
- 2 cloves garlic, minced
- 1/2 tsp. dried basil
- Salt and black pepper, to taste
- Fresh chopped parsley, for garnish

Instructions

1. Turn on the 375°F oven.
2. Balsamic vinegar, olive oil, honey, garlic, basil, salt, and black pepper should all be combined in a small bowl.
3. A big baking dish should be used for the chicken breasts. Pour the balsamic mixture over the top, being sure to cover each breast completely.
4. Bake the chicken for 25 to 30 minutes or until it is well-cooked and the center is no longer pink.
5. After taking the chicken out of the oven, let it five minutes to rest.
6. Serve hot and garnish with freshly chopped parsley.

CHAPTER 4: DINNER RECIPES

Healthy Chicken Salad

Serving: 4

Preparation time: 10 minutes

Cooking time: 0 minutes.

Ingredients

- 2 cups of cooked chicken, shredded
- 1/2 cup of plain Greek yogurt
- 1/4 cup of diced red onion
- 1/4 cup of diced celery
- 1/4 cup of diced apple
- 1/4 cup of chopped walnuts
- 1 tbsp. Dijon mustard
- 1 tbsp. lemon juice
- 1 tsp. honey
- Salt and black pepper, to taste
- Lettuce leaves for serving

Instructions

1. The cooked chicken, Greek yogurt, red onion, celery, apple, and walnuts should all be combined in a big bowl.
2. Mix the Dijon mustard, honey, lemon juice, salt, and black pepper in a small bowl.
3. Mix the chicken mixture with the dressing after pouring it over it.
4. Over lettuce leaves, serve the chicken salad.

Skillet Quinoa

Serving: 4

Preparation time: 10 minutes

Cooking time: 25 minutes.

Ingredients

- 1 cup of quinoa, rinsed
- 1 tablespoon olive oil
- 1 small onion, diced
- 3 cloves garlic, minced
- 1 red bell pepper, diced
- 1 yellow bell pepper, diced
- 1 teaspoon ground cumin
- 1/2 teaspoon smoked paprika
- 1/4 teaspoon cayenne pepper
- 2 cups of vegetable broth
- Salt and black pepper, to taste
- Fresh cilantro leaves, chopped, for serving

Instructions

1. Over medium heat, warm the olive oil in a large skillet.
2. For approximately 5 minutes, add the onion and garlic and sauté until tender.
3. Red and yellow bell peppers should be added and cooked for 3–4 minutes or until just softened.
4. Stir in the cumin, smoked paprika, cayenne pepper, and quinoa after adding them.
5. Add the veggie broth, then mix once more.
6. After the mixture has reached a rolling boil, turn the heat down to low and cover the skillet.
7. When the quinoa is cooked, and the majority of the liquid has been absorbed, simmer for 15 to 20 minutes.
8. To taste, add salt and black pepper to the food.
9. Before serving, garnish with fresh cilantro leaves.

Zucchini Potato Stew

Servings: 4-6

Preparation Time: 10 minutes

Cooking Time: 35 minutes

Ingredients:

- 2 tablespoons olive oil
- 1 onion, chopped
- 2 cloves garlic, minced
- 4 medium potatoes, peeled and diced
- 2 medium zucchinis, diced
- 14 oz diced tomatoes, undrained
- 2 cups of vegetable broth
- 1 teaspoon dried oregano
- 1 teaspoon dried basil
- Salt and pepper to taste

Instructions

1. Heat the olive oil over medium heat in a big pan or Dutch oven.
2. Cook the onion and garlic together for approximately 5 minutes or until the onion is tender and transparent.
3. Including their liquids, add the cubed potatoes, zucchini, and tomatoes.
4. Salt, pepper, oregano, basil, and vegetable broth should all be added.
5. To thoroughly incorporate all the ingredients, stir well.
6. Bring the mixture to boil. Turn down the heat.
7. For about 25 to 30 minutes, or until the potatoes are fully cooked and soft, boil the stew with the cover on.
8. If required, taste and adjust the seasoning.
9. Warm zucchini-potato stew should be served alongside some crusty bread.

Potatoes with Beans

Servings: 4

Preparation time: 15 minutes

Cooking time: 35 minutes

Ingredients

- 4 medium-sized potatoes, peeled and cut into small cubes
- 1 can drained and rinsedof black beans,
- 1 red onion, chopped
- 1 red bell pepper, chopped
- 2 cloves of garlic, minced
- 2 tablespoons of olive oil
- 1 teaspoon of ground cumin
- 1/2 teaspoon of smoked paprika
- Salt and black pepper, to taste
- 2 tablespoons of chopped fresh cilantro
- Juice of 1 lime

Instructions

1. Over medium-high heat, warm the olive oil in a large skillet. For 3–4 minutes, until softened, add the chopped onion and bell pepper.
2. Cook for a further one to two minutes, often stirring, after adding the minced garlic, ground cumin, and smoky paprika.
3. The potatoes should be added to the skillet and cooked for 20 to 25 minutes, turning periodically or until they are soft and lightly browned.
4. Black beans should be heated through after being added and cooked for an additional 5-7 minutes.
5. Add salt and black pepper according to taste.
6. Add the chopped cilantro and lime juice after turning off the heat.
7. Serve hot with grilled fish or poultry as a side dish

.

Easy Shrimp Scampi

Servings: 4

Preparation time: 10 minutes

Cooking time: 15 minutes

Ingredients:

- 1 pound medium shrimp, peeled and deveined
- 4 cloves garlic, minced
- 1/2 teaspoon red pepper flakes
- 1/2 cup of dry white wine
- 1/4 cup of freshly squeezed lemon juice
- 4 tablespoons unsalted butter
- 2 tablespoons olive oil
- 1/4 cup of chopped fresh parsley
- Salt and freshly ground black pepper
- 12 ounces linguine, cooked according to package instructions
- Parmesan cheese, grated, for serving

Instructions:

1. In a large pan over medium-high heat, melt the butter and 2 tablespoons of olive oil.
2. Cook for 30 seconds after adding the red pepper flakes and garlic.
3. Add the shrimp and fry for 2-3 minutes per side until pink and cooked through. The shrimp should be taken out of the pan and put aside.
4. Bring the white wine and lemon juice to a simmer in the pan. Sauté for a further 2 to 3 minutes or until the liquid is cut in half.
5. Next, add the remaining 2 tablespoons of butter and whisk until it has melted.
6. Add the chopped parsley and bring the shrimp back to the skillet. Mix everything together until the sauce is evenly distributed over the shrimp.
7. Add salt and freshly ground black pepper to taste when preparing the shrimp scampi.
8. Sprinkle-grated Parmesan cheese over the prepared linguine before serving the shrimp scampi.

Greek Salmon

Serving: 4

Preparation time: 10 minutes

Cooking time: 15 minutes

Ingredients:

- 4 salmon fillets (6 ounces each)
- 1/4 cup of olive oil
- 1/4 cup of freshly squeezed lemon juice
- 2 cloves garlic, minced
- 1 teaspoon dried oregano
- 1 teaspoon dried thyme
- 1/2 teaspoon salt
- 1/4 teaspoon black pepper
- 1/2 cup of chopped kalamata olives
- 1/2 cup of crumbled feta cheese
- 1/4 cup of chopped fresh parsley

Instructions:

1. Set the oven's temperature to 400°F (200°C).
2. Mix the olive oil, thyme, salt, lemon juice, garlic, oregano, and black pepper in a small bowl.
3. Salmon fillets should be placed skin-side down in a baking dish. Be careful to cover each fillet of salmon with a combination of olive oil.
4. Over the salmon fillets, strew the feta cheese crumbles and chopped olives.
5. Bake the salmon for 12 to 15 minutes.
6. The salmon should be served hot with the parsley cut on top.

Spicy Grilled Shrimp

Servings: 4

Preparation Time: 10 minutes

Cooking Time: 6-8 minutes

Ingredients

- 1 lb large shrimp, peeled and deveined
- 2 cloves garlic, minced
- 2 tbsp olive oil
- 1 tbsp honey
- 1 tbsp smoked paprika
- 1 tsp cayenne pepper
- 1 tsp salt
- 1/2 tsp black pepper
- 1 lemon, juiced

Instructions

1. Heat the grill to medium-high.
2. Mix the garlic, olive oil, honey, smoked paprika, cayenne, salt, black pepper, and lemon juice in a small bowl.
3. Skewers are threaded with shrimp.
4. Making ensuring they are thoroughly covered, brush the marinade over the shrimp skewers.
5. Grill shrimp for two to three minutes on each side or until they are fully cooked and have developed a little sear.
6. If preferred, top with fresh parsley or cilantro and serve hot with lemon wedges.

Baked Cod

Serving: 4 servings.

Preparation time: 5-10 minutes

Cooking time: 15-20 minutes

Ingredients

- 4 cod fillets
- 1/4 cup of olive oil
- 1 lemon, juiced
- 2 cloves garlic, minced
- 1 tsp dried oregano
- Salt and pepper to taste
- Lemon wedges and parsley for garnish

Instructions

1. Turn on the 375°F oven.
2. Mix the olive oil, lemon juice, minced garlic, dried oregano, salt, and pepper in a small bowl.
3. Put the fish fillets on a baking tray and pour the marinade over them. Ensure that each fillet is well coated.
4. Bake for 15 to 20 minutes in a preheated oven or until the cod flakes easily with a fork.
5. Serve hot with garnishes of parsley and lemon wedges.

Herb Shrimp

Serving: 4

Preparation time: 10 minutes

Cooking time: 10-12 minutes

Ingredients

- 1 pound shrimp, peeled and deveined
- 2 tablespoons olive oil
- 2 tablespoons chopped fresh herbs
- 2 cloves garlic, minced
- Salt and pepper to taste

Instructions

1. Set the oven to 400 °F.
2. Olive oil, chopped herbs, minced garlic, salt, and pepper should all be combined in a small bowl.
3. On a baking dish, arrange the shrimp in a single layer.
4. Sprinkle the shrimp with the herb mixture, tossing to coat well.
5. Bake shrimp for 10 to 12 minutes or until they are fully cooked and pink.
6. Serve hot alongside your preferred side dish.

Lemon Garlic Chicken Tenders

Servings: 4

Preparation time: 15 minutes

Cooking time: 20 minutes

Ingredients

- 1 lb chicken tenders
- 1/2 cup of all-purpose flour
- 1 tsp salt
- 1/2 tsp black pepper
- 2 tbsp olive oil
- 2 tbsp butter
- 4 garlic cloves, minced
- 1/4 cup of chicken broth
- 1/4 cup of freshly squeezed lemon juice
- 1/4 cup of chopped fresh parsley

Preparation

1. Set the oven's temperature to 400°F (200°C).
2. Combine the flour, salt, and black pepper in a small bowl.
3. Each chicken tender should be well covered in the flour mixture.
4. In a large skillet over medium-high heat, warm the olive oil.
5. After the chicken tenders are added, grill them for 3–4 minutes on each side or until they are well cooked.
6. The chicken tenders should be taken out of the pan and put in a baking dish.
7. Melt the butter over medium heat in the same skillet.
8. After the garlic is aromatic, add it and simmer for one to two minutes.
9. Stir together the chicken broth and lemon juice in the skillet after adding them.
10. The chicken tenders in the baking dish should be covered with lemon-garlic sauce.
11. Bake the chicken for 10 to 12 minutes or until it is well done.
12. Before serving, add some chopped parsley as a garnish.

Thyme Chicken with Mushrooms

Serving: 4 servings

Preparation time: 15 minutes

Cooking time: 35 minutes

Ingredients:

- 4 boneless, skinless chicken breasts
- 2 cups of sliced mushrooms
- 1/4 cup of all-purpose flour
- 1 tsp dried thyme
- 1/2 tsp salt
- 1/4 tsp black pepper
- 2 tbsp olive oil
- 2 tbsp butter
- 1/2 cup of chicken broth
- 1/2 cup of dry white wine
- 1/4 cup of chopped fresh parsley

Directions:

1. The oven heated to 375°F (190°C).
2. Combine the flour, thyme, salt, and pepper in a small basin.
3. Each chicken breast should be well coated in the flour mixture.
4. Over medium-high heat, warm up the olive oil in a big skillet. Add the chicken breasts and brown for 3 to 4 minutes on each side. Place chicken in a baking dish after removing it from the pan.
5. Sliced mushrooms should be added to the skillet and cooked for 2 to 3 minutes. Save the mushrooms from the skillet for later.
6. Melt the butter in the skillet after adding it. Add the flour and whisk continuously for 1–2 minutes. White wine and chicken broth should be whisked in gradually to get a smooth consistency.
7. Over the chicken breasts in the baking dish, pour the sauce. Add the mushrooms on top.
8. Bake the chicken for 25-30 minute or until it is well cooked, and the sauce is bubbling.
9. Before serving, top with chopped parsley.

Easy Mediterranean Chicken

Serving: 4

Preparation time: 10 minutes

Cooking time: 30 minutes

Ingredients

- 4 chicken breasts, boneless and skinless
- 2 tbsp olive oil
- 2 tsp paprika
- 1 tsp garlic powder
- 1 tsp onion powder
- 1 tsp dried oregano
- 1 tsp dried thyme
- Salt and pepper to taste
- 1 cup of cherry tomatoes, halved
- 1/2 cup of kalamata olives, pitted and halved
- 1/4 cup of crumbled feta cheese
- 1/4 cup of chopped fresh parsley

Directions:

1. A 375°F (190°C) oven is to be preheated.
2. Olive oil, paprika, onion powder, garlic powder, thyme, oregano, salt, and pepper should all be combined in a small basin.
3. The olive oil mixture should be brushed over the chicken breasts after placing them in a baking dish.
4. Scattered around the chicken, add cherry tomatoes and kalamata olives to the dish.
5. The chicken should be fully cooked, with an internal temperature of 165°F (74°C), after 25 to 30 minutes in the oven.
6. Sprinkle feta cheese crumbles and chopped parsley on top after removing them from the oven.
7. Enjoy when still hot!

Flavors Chicken Skewers:

Serving: 4

Preparation time: 15 minutes

Marinating time: 30 minutes

Cooking time: 10-12 minutes

Ingredients:

- 4 boneless, skinless chicken breasts
- 1/4 cup of olive oil
- 3 cloves garlic, minced
- 2 tbsp chopped fresh parsley
- 1 tbsp chopped fresh thyme
- 1 tbsp chopped fresh oregano
- 1 tsp salt
- 1/2 tsp black pepper
- Juice of 1 lemon
- Wooden skewers soaked in water for at least 28 minutes

Instructions:

1. Mix the olive oil, garlic, parsley, thyme, oregano, salt, black pepper, and lemon juice in a large bowl.
2. Toss the chicken in the marinade after adding it to the bowl. Refrigerate the bowl for at least 30 minutes or for as long as 2 hours, covered with plastic wrap.
3. Set the temperature of your grill or grill pan to medium-high.
4. The skewers are threaded with chunks of chicken.
5. The chicken skewers should be cooked through after 5 to 6 minutes on each side of the grill.
6. Serve warm.

Vegetable Bean Gumbo

Servings: 6

Preparation time: 20 minutes

Cooking time: 1 hour

Ingredients:

- 2 tablespoons olive oil
- 1 onion, chopped
- 3 garlic cloves, minced
- 1 green bell pepper, chopped
- 2 celery stalks, chopped
- 14.5 oz diced tomatoes, undrained
- 15 oz kidney beans, rinsed and drained
- 15 oz black beans, rinsed and drained
- 4 cups of vegetable broth
- 1 tablespoon tomato paste
- 2 teaspoons dried thyme
- 2 teaspoons dried oregano
- 1 teaspoon paprika
- 1/2 teaspoon cayenne pepper
- Salt and pepper to taste
- Cooked rice or quinoa for serving

Instructions

1. Over medium heat, heat the olive oil in a large saucepan.
2. Sauté the onion and garlic for 2-3 minutes, until translucent.
3. Sauté the celery and green bell pepper for 3-4 minutes more, until they soften.
4. Mix in the tomatoes, kidney beans, and black beans. Add tomato paste, tomato paste, tomato paste thyme oregano.
5. Bring the mixture to a boil. Then reduce heat to simmer for 45-50 mins until vegetables are tender and flavors have melded.
6. Serve the vegetable bean soup over cooked rice or quinoa.

CHAPTER 5: SNACKS & SIDES

Roasted Potatoes

Serving: 4-6 people.

Preparation time: 10 minutes

Cooking time: 30-40 minutes.

Ingredients:

- 2 lbs potatoes, washed and cut into bite-sized pieces
- 2 tbsp olive oil
- 1 tsp salt
- 1/2 tsp black pepper
- 1 tsp garlic powder
- 1 tsp paprika

Instructions

1. Preheat the oven to 400°F.
2. Toss the potatoes in salt,olive oil, and black pepper with garlic powder until well coated.
3. Place the potatoes in one layer on a parchment-lined baking sheet.
4. The potatoes should be roasted for between 30-40 minutes. Stir the potatoes once or twice throughout the cooking process until they become crispy on the outside and soft on the inside.
5. If desired, serve the potatoes warm with chopped parsley and chives.

Easy Chickpea Roast

Servings: 4

Preparation Time: 10 minutes

Cooking Time: 25 minutes

Ingredients:

- 2 cans chickpeas, drained and rinsed
- 2 tablespoons olive oil
- 2 cloves garlic, minced
- 1 teaspoon smoked paprika
- 1/2 teaspoon cumin
- 1/2 teaspoon salt
- Freshly ground black pepper
- Lemon wedges for serving

Instructions:

1. Preheat the oven to 400°F.
2. Mix the chickpeas with olive oil, garlic, cumin, and smoked paprika in a large bowl.
3. Spread the chickpea mix in a single layer onto a baking sheet.
4. Bake for between 20-25 minutes, stirring halfway through, or until chickpeas turn golden brown.
5. Hot chickpeas with lemon wedges served on the side.

Roasted Zucchini & Cauliflower

Serving: 4 servings.

Preparation time: 10 minutes

Cooking time: 25-30 minutes

Ingredients:

- 1 medium head of cauliflower, chopped into bite-size pieces
- 2 medium zucchinis, chopped into bite-size pieces
- 2 tbsp olive oil
- 1 tsp garlic powder
- 1 tsp dried thyme
- 1/2 tsp salt
- 1/4 tsp black pepper

Instructions:

1. Preheat the oven to 425°F. Line a baking sheet using parchment paper.
2. Combine the zucchini and cauliflower in a large bowl.
3. Toss the vegetables in the olive oil and mix well.
4. Toss the chopped garlic, thyme, and salt with the pepper until all the spices are well coated.
5. Place the vegetables in one layer on the baking sheet.
6. Bake in the oven for between 25-30 minutes or until vegetables are tender. Toss once halfway through.
7. Enjoy hot!

Potatoes with Cheese

Serving: 4-6 people.

Preparation time: 15 minutes

Cooking time: 45 minutes

Ingredients

- 4-5 medium-sized potatoes, peeled and sliced into rounds
- 1 cup of shredded cheddar cheese
- 1/2 cup of grated Parmesan cheese
- 1/2 cup of heavy cream
- 2 cloves garlic, minced
- 1/4 cup of chopped fresh parsley
- Salt and pepper to taste
- 2 tablespoons butter

Instructions

1. Preheat oven to 375°F (190°C).
2. Melt the butter in a saucepan on medium heat and saute garlic till fragrant.
3. Stir in the cream. Let it simmer for a while until it becomes slightly thickened.
4. Stir in the cheddar cheese until it is melted.
5. Butter or cooking spray can be used to grease a baking dish.
6. Place a layer of potatoes on the bottom of your dish. Season with salt and pepper.
7. Place half the cheese sauce on top of the potatoes.
8. Continue with the second layer of potatoes and the remaining cheese sauce.
9. Sprinkle the Parmesan cheese on top.
10. Bake the dish for 30 minutes, covered with foil.
11. Bake for an additional 12-15 minutes, or until potatoes are tender and cheese is golden brown.
12. Serve hot with fresh parsley.

Healthy Green Beans

Serving: 4 servings

Preparation time: 10 minutes

Cooking time: 15-20 minutes

Ingredients:

- 1 pound fresh green beans, ends trimmed
- 2 tablespoons olive oil
- 2 garlic cloves, minced
- 1/2 teaspoon salt
- 1/4 teaspoon black pepper

Instructions

1. Preheat the oven to 425°F.
2. Toss the green beans in garlic, salt, olive oil, and pepper in a large bowl until well coated.
3. Place the green beans in one layer on a large baking tray.
4. Bake in the oven for 17-20 minutes or until tender and lightly browned. Stir halfway through.
5. Enjoy hot!

Rosemary Carrots

Servings: 4

Preparation time: 10 minutes

Cooking time: 25-30 minutes

Ingredients:

- 1 pound carrots, peeled and sliced diagonally
- 1 tablespoon olive oil
- 1 tablespoon fresh rosemary, chopped
- Salt and black pepper, to taste

Instructions:

1. Preheat the oven to 400°F
2. Toss the sliced carrots in olive oil, chopped rosemary, salt, and black pepper in a bowl.
3. Place the carrots on a baking sheet or dish and arrange them in one layer.
4. Roast the carrots in the oven for between 25-30 minutes or until they are tender.
5. As a side dish, serve the roasted carrots hot.

Tuna Patties

Serving: 4 patties

Preparation time: 10 minutes

Cooking time: 10 minutes

Ingredients:

- 2 cans of tuna, drained
- 1/2 cup of breadcrumbs
- 1/4 cup of finely chopped onion
- 1/4 cup of finely chopped celery
- 1/4 cup of mayonnaise
- 2 tablespoons Dijon mustard
- 1 teaspoon garlic powder
- 1 teaspoon dried dill
- Salt and pepper to taste
- 2 tablespoons olive oil

Instructions

1. Combine the tuna, breadcrumbs, onion, celery and mayonnaise in a large bowl. Add garlic powder, Dijon mustard, dried dill, salt and pepper. Combine all ingredients well.
2. Make four equal-sized patties from the mixture.
3. Place the olive oil in an oven-proof skillet on medium heat.
4. Once the skillet has heaved, add the tuna patties. Cook for about 3-5 minutes or until golden brown.
5. To remove excess oil from the pan, place the patties on a towel.
6. Serve warm with your favorite dipping sauces or toppings, such as tartar sauce, lemon juice or a squeeze of lime juice. Enjoy!

Quick Parsnips

Servings: 4

Preparation time: 10 minutes

Cooking time: 15-20 minutes

Ingredients

- 1 pound parsnips, peeled and cut into 1-inch pieces
- 2 tablespoons olive oil
- 1 teaspoon dried thyme
- 1 teaspoon garlic powder
- Salt and pepper to taste

Instructions

1. Preheat the oven to 400°F.
2. Toss the parsnips in olive oil, garlic powder, salt and pepper in a bowl.
3. Place the chopped parsnips in one layer on a baking tray.
4. Bake the parsnips in the oven for about 15-20 minutes or until tender and lightly browned.
5. As a side dish, serve the parsnips with your favorite main meal.

Rosemary Almonds:

Serving: 2 cups of

Preparation time: 5 minutes

Cooking time: 10-15 minutes.

Ingredients

- 2 cups of whole raw almonds
- 1 tablespoon olive oil
- 1 tablespoon finely chopped fresh rosemary leaves
- 1/2 teaspoon garlic powder
- 1/2 teaspoon sea salt

Instructions:

1. Preheat oven to 350°F
2. Combine the olive oil, almonds, rosemary, garlic powder, and sea salt in a bowl. Mix to coat all the almonds.
3. Place the almonds in one layer on a parchment-lined baking sheet.
4. Bake the almonds for about 10-15 minutes until they are fragrant and golden brown.
5. Let the almonds cool in the oven for at least 30 minutes before removing the baking sheet.

Baked Zucchini Chips

Serving size: 4

Preparation time: 10 minutes

Cooking time: 20-25 minutes

Ingredients

- 2 medium zucchinis
- 1/2 cup of all-purpose flour
- 2 eggs
- 1 cup of panko breadcrumbs
- 1/4 cup of grated Parmesan cheese
- 1/2 teaspoon garlic powder
- 1/2 teaspoon paprika
- Salt and pepper, to taste
- Cooking spray

Instructions

1. Preheat oven to 425degF.
2. Cut the zucchinis into rounds about 1/4 inch thick.
3. In a small bowl, combine the flour and water. Mix the eggs in a separate bowl. Mix the eggs in a third bowl. Add the panko breadcrumbs and Parmesan cheese to the bowl. Season with salt and pepper.
4. Each zucchini should be dipped in flour, followed by egg and breadcrumbs.
5. Place the breaded zucchini rounds onto a parchment-lined baking sheet.
6. Spray the zucchini chips using cooking spray.
7. Bake the chips for between 10-12 minutes or until they are lightly browned. Bake the chips for 10-12 minutes or until they are crispy and golden brown.
8. Allow cooling in the oven before taking it out. Serve as a side or snack.

Brussels Sprouts with Cheese

Servings: 4

Preparation time: 10 minutes

Cooking time: 20 minutes

Ingredients

- 1 lb Brussels sprouts, trimmed and halved
- 2 tbsp olive oil
- 1 tsp garlic powder
- Salt and pepper, to taste
- 1/2 cup of grated Parmesan cheese
- 1/4 cup of panko breadcrumbs

Instructions

1. Preheat your oven to 400°F.
2. Mix the olive oil, garlic powder, and salt in a large bowl until well coated.
3. Place the Brussels sprouts in one layer on a baking tray.
4. Bake the Brussels sprouts in the oven for 15-20 minutes or until tender and lightly browned.
5. Mix the panko breadcrumbs and Parmesan cheese in a small bowl.
6. Sprinkle the Parmesan mix over the Brussels sprouts.
7. Bake the sheet in the oven for another 5-7 minutes or until it is bubbly and melted.
8. Serve immediately.

Cheese Roasted Cauliflower

Serving: 4 servings.

Preparation time: 10 minutes

Cooking time: 25-30 minutes

Ingredients

- 1 head cauliflower, cut into florets
- 2 tablespoons olive oil
- Salt and black pepper to taste
- 1/2 teaspoon garlic powder
- 1/2 cup of shredded cheddar cheese
- 1/4 cup of grated Parmesan cheese

Instructions

1. Preheat oven to 400°F (200°C).
2. Put cauliflower florets into a large bowl. Drizzle olive oil over them. Mix to coat.
3. Toss the mixture with salt, black pepper, and garlic powder, and again.
4. Place the cauliflower in one layer on a baking tray.
5. Bake for between 20-25 minutes or until cauliflower is tender.
6. After removing the cauliflower from the oven, top it with the Parmesan and cheddar cheeses.
7. Bake for another 5-7 minutes or until the cheese is melted.
8. Serve immediately.

Baked Sweet Potatoes

Serving: 4

Preparation time: 5 minutes

Cooking time: 45-60 minutes

Ingredients

- 4 medium sweet potatoes
- 2 tbsp olive oil
- 1 tsp salt
- 1/2 tsp black pepper
- Optional toppings: butter, brown sugar, chopped nuts, cinnamon

Instructions

1. Preheat the oven to 400°F.
2. Pat the sweet potatoes dry after washing them.
3. Use a fork to poke each potato multiple times.
4. Use olive oil to rub each potato, and then sprinkle salt and pepper on top.
5. Bake the potatoes on a baking tray for 45-60 minutes or until tender when pierced using a fork.
6. Remove the cake from the oven and give it some time to cool.
7. Each potato should be cut in half lengthwise. Fluff the inside with a fork.
8. You can add any toppings you like, butter, brown sugar, or chopped nuts, as well as cinnamon.
9. Enjoy your delicious baked sweet potatoes!

Roasted Brussels Sprouts with Garlic and Parmesan

Servings: 4-6

Preparation time: 10 minutes

Cooking time: 20-25 minutes

Ingredients

- 1 lb Brussels sprouts, trimmed and halved
- 3 cloves garlic, minced
- 3 tbsp olive oil
- 1/2 tsp salt
- 1/4 tsp black pepper
- 1/4 cup of grated Parmesan cheese

Directions

1. Preheat oven to 400°F
2. Mix together the Brussels sprouts with olive oil, garlic, salt, and pepper in a bowl.
3. Place the Brussels sprouts in one layer on a baking sheet.
4. Bake for between 20-25 minutes or until the meat is tender and lightly browned.
5. Sprinkle with Parmesan cheese, and serve.

CHAPTER 6: SOUPS & SALADS

Classic Tomato Soup

Servings: 4

Preparation time: 5 minutes

Cooking time: 15-20 minutes

Ingredients

- 2 tbsp butter
- 1 onion, diced
- 2 cloves garlic, minced
- 2 cans (14.5 oz each) of diced tomatoes
- 2 cups of chicken or vegetable broth
- 1/2 cup of heavy cream
- Salt and pepper, to taste

Directions

1. Melt the butter in a large saucepan over medium heat.
2. Cook the garlic and onion for about five minutes.
3. Bring to a boil the broth and diced tomatoes.
4. Let the soup simmer for about 10-15 minutes until the tomatoes are broken down, and the soup thickens slightly.
5. Blend the soup using an immersion blender.
6. Add the heavy cream to the bowl and season with salt & pepper. Serve immediately.

Kale Quinoa Salad with Lemon Vinaigrette

Servings: 4

Preparation time: 15 minutes

Cooking time: 20-25 minutes

Ingredients

- 1 cup of quinoa, rinsed
- 2 cups of water
- 1 bunch of kale, stems removed and leaves chopped
- 1/2 red onion, thinly sliced
- 1/2 cup of sliced almonds
- 1/2 cup of crumbled feta cheese
- 1/4 cup of olive oil
- 3 tbsp fresh lemon juice
- 2 tsp honey
- Salt and pepper, to taste

Directions

1. Combine the quinoa with water in a large saucepan. Bring to a boil. Reduce heat to low, and simmer for 20-25 mins or until quinoa is tender.
2. Combine the cooked quinoa and kale with red onion, red onions, almonds, and feta in a large bowl.
3. Mix the olive oil with lemon juice, honey, salt, and pepper in a small bowl.
4. Toss the salad in the dressing and mix well. Serve chilled or at room temperature.

Zucchini Ribbon Salad with Feta and Mint

Servings: 4

Preparation time: 15 minutes

Cooking time: none

Ingredients

- 2 medium zucchini, washed and ends trimmed
- 1/4 cup of crumbled feta cheese
- 2 tbsp chopped fresh mint leaves
- 2 tbsp olive oil
- 1 tbsp fresh lemon juice
- Salt and pepper, to taste

Directions

1. Use a mandoline or vegetable peeler to cut the zucchini into thin strips.
2. Combine the chopped mint, zucchini ribbons, and feta cheese in a large bowl.
3. Mix the olive oil, lemon zest, salt and pepper in a small bowl.
4. Toss the salad in the dressing and mix well. Serve immediately.

Spinach and White Bean Soup

Servings: 4

Preparation time: 10 minutes

Cooking time: 25-30 minutes

Ingredients:

- 2 tbsp olive oil
- 1 onion, chopped
- 2 cloves garlic, minced
- 4 cups of vegetable broth
- 15 oz each of white beans, drained and rinsed
- 1 tsp dried thyme
- 1/4 tsp red pepper flakes
- 4 cups of fresh spinach
- Salt and pepper, to taste

Directions

1. Heat the olive oil in a saucepan on medium heat. Cook the onion and garlic for 5 minutes.
2. The vegetable broth, white beans and thyme should be added to the pot. Reduce heat to medium and simmer for about 15-20 minute.
3. Mix roughly half the soup with an immersion blender.
4. Add the fresh spinach to the pot and continue cooking for 5-10 minutes until it is wilted.
5. Salt and pepper to your liking. Serve hot.

Classic Vegetable Soup

Servings: 6-8

Preparation time: 20 minutes

Cooking time: 30-40 minutes

Ingredients

- 2 tbsp olive oil
- 1 onion, chopped
- 2 cloves garlic, minced
- 2 carrots, peeled and chopped
- 2 celery stalks, chopped
- 1 zucchini, chopped
- 1 yellow squash, chopped
- 1 can (28 oz) diced tomatoes
- 4 cups of vegetable broth
- 1 tsp dried oregano
- 1 tsp dried basil
- Salt and pepper, to taste

Directions

1. Heat the olive oil in a large saucepan on medium heat. Cook the onion and garlic for 5 minutes.
2. Cook the yellow squash, carrots, celery and celery for another 5-10 minutes until tender.
3. To the pot, add the chopped tomatoes, vegetable broth and oregano, basil, salt and pepper. Turn the heat to low and let it simmer for about 15-20 minutes.
4. Serve hot.

Classic Chicken Salad

Servings: 4-6

Preparation time: 15 minutes

Cooking time: 15-20 minutes

Ingredients

- 2 boneless, skinless chicken breasts
- 1/2 cup of mayonnaise
- 1/4 cup of chopped celery
- 1/4 cup of chopped red onion
- 1/4 cup of chopped fresh parsley
- 1 tbsp lemon juice
- Salt and pepper, to taste

Directions

1. Preheat the oven to 400°F. Season the breasts of the chicken with salt and pepper. Roast for 15-20 minutes until they are cooked through.
2. Let the chicken cool and then cut it into small pieces.
3. Combine the mayonnaise, celery and red onion with the chicken. Add the lemon juice, salt, pepper, parsley, and lemon juice to a large bowl.
4. Combine all ingredients well. Serve chilled.

Watermelon Feta Salad

Servings: 4

Preparation time: 15 minutes

Cooking time: None

Ingredients

- 4 cups of cubed watermelon
- 1/2 cup of crumbled feta cheese
- 1/4 cup of chopped fresh mint
- 2 tbsp extra-virgin olive oil
- 1 tbsp balsamic vinegar
- Salt and pepper, to taste

Directions

1. Combine the watermelon, feta, and mint in a large bowl.
2. Combine the olive oil and balsamic vinegar in a small bowl. Toss the mixture with watermelon and olive oil.
3. Salt and pepper to your liking. Serve chilled.

Classic Potato, Tuna, and Bean Salad

Servings: 4-6

Preparation time: 20 minutes

Cooking time: 15-20 minutes

Ingredients

- 1 lb potatoes, cut into small cubes
- 15 oz cannellini beans, drained and rinsed
- 5 oz tuna, drained
- 1/4 cup of chopped red onion
- 1/4 cup of chopped fresh parsley
- 1/4 cup of olive oil
- 2 tbsp red wine vinegar
- Salt and pepper, to taste

Directions:

1. Cook the potatoes in a large saucepan of boiling salted water until they are tender (about 15-20 minutes). Let cool.
2. Combine the tuna, red onions, tuna and cannellini beans in a large bowl.
3. Mix the olive oil, and red wine vinegar in a small bowl. Toss the potato mixture with olive oil and red wine vinegar.
4. Salt and pepper to your liking. Serve chilled.

Classic Black Bean Salad

Servings: 4-6

Preparation time: 15 minutes

Cooking time: None

Ingredients:

- 15 oz black beans, drained and rinsed
- 1 cup of diced tomatoes
- 1 cup of diced red onion
- 1/2 cup of chopped fresh cilantro
- 2 tbsp lime juice
- 2 tbsp olive oil
- 1 tsp ground cumin
- Salt and pepper, to taste

Directions:

1. Combine the black beans with tomatoes, red onions, and cilantro in a large bowl.
2. Mix together the lime juice and olive oil with the cumin, salt, pepper, and salt in a small bowl. Toss the bean mixture with olive oil and cumin.
3. Serve chilled.

Tuna White Bean Salad

Serves: 4

Preparation time: 15 minutes

Ingredients:

- 2 cans of white beans,
- 2 cans of tuna, drained and flaked
- 1/2 red onion, finely chopped
- 1/2 cup of cherry tomatoes, halved
- 1/4 cup of chopped fresh parsley
- 2 tablespoons of lemon juice
- 2 tablespoons of olive oil
- Salt and pepper to taste

Instructions:

1. Combine the white beans with tuna, tuna, red onions, cherry tomatoes and parsley in a large bowl.
2. Mix the lemon juice, olive oils, salt and pepper in a small bowl.
3. Toss the salad in the dressing and mix well.
4. Serve immediately, or keep in the refrigerator until ready to use.

Healthy Lentil Salad

Serves: 4

Preparation time: 20 minutes

Cooking time: 20 minutes

Ingredients:

- 1 cup of green or brown lentils, rinsed and drained
- 2 cups of water or vegetable broth
- 1 red bell pepper, diced
- 1 small red onion, diced
- 1 cup of cherry tomatoes, halved
- 1/4 cup of chopped fresh parsley
- 1/4 cup of chopped fresh mint
- 1/4 cup of crumbled feta cheese (optional)
- 1/4 cup of extra-virgin olive oil
- 2 tablespoons of red wine vinegar
- 1 garlic clove, minced
- Salt and pepper to taste

Instructions:

1. Combine the lentils with the water or broth in a large saucepan. Bring to a boil. Reduce heat to low and simmer for between 20-25 minutes or until lentils become tender but not mushy. Get rid of any extra water.
2. Combine the red bell pepper, red onions, cherry tomatoes and cooked lentils in a large bowl. Add the parsley and mint.
3. Mix the olive oil with red wine vinegar, garlic, salt and pepper in a small bowl.
4. Toss the salad in the dressing and mix well.
5. Sprinkle feta cheese on the salad before serving.
6. Serve immediately, or keep in the refrigerator until ready to use.

Colorful Bean Salad:

Serving: 6-8 people.

Preparation time: 15 minutes.

Cooking time:

Ingredients:

- 1 can black beans, rinsed and drained
- 1 can kidney beans, rinsed and drained
- 1 can chickpeas, rinsed and drained
- 1 red bell pepper, diced
- 1 yellow bell pepper, diced
- 1/2 red onion, diced
- 1/4 cup of fresh cilantro, chopped
- 1 avocado, diced
- Juice of 1 lime
- 2 tablespoons olive oil
- Salt and pepper to taste

Instructions:

1. Combine the black beans, kidney beans and chickpeas in a large bowl.
2. Then add the red bell pepper, yellow bell pepper, and red onions to the bowl.
3. Add the chopped cilantro and diced avocado and mix.
4. Mix the olive oil and lime juice in a small bowl. Toss the salad with the dressing and mix well.
5. Salt and pepper to your liking
6. To allow flavors to blend, chill the salad at least 30 minutes prior to serving.

Classic Tuna Salad

Serving Size: 2-3

Preparation Time: 10 minutes

Ingredients:

- 2 cans of solid white albacore tuna, drained
- 1/3 cup of mayonnaise
- 2 tbsp finely chopped red onion
- 2 tbsp chopped celery
- 1 tbsp fresh lemon juice
- Salt and pepper to taste
- Optional: chopped parsley for garnish

Directions:

1. Mix the tuna, mayonnaise and red onion with celery in a large bowl. Add lemon juice.
2. Salt and pepper to your liking
3. To allow flavors to blend, cover and place in the refrigerator for at least 30 min.
4. If desired, serve cold and garnish with chopped parsley.

Chickpea Salad

Servings: 4

Preparation Time: 15 minutes

Cooking Time: 0 minutes

Ingredients

- 2 cans chickpeas, drained and rinsed
- 1 red bell pepper, chopped
- 1/2 red onion, chopped
- 1 cup of cherry tomatoes, halved
- 1/4 cup of chopped fresh parsley
- 1/4 cup of chopped fresh mint
- 1/4 cup of extra-virgin olive oil
- 2 tablespoons red wine vinegar
- 1 clove garlic, minced
- Salt and black pepper, to taste

Instructions

1. Combine the chickpeas with red bell pepper, red onions, cherry tomatoes and parsley in a large bowl.
2. Mix the olive oil with red wine vinegar, garlic, salt and black pepper in a small bowl.
3. Toss the dressing over the chickpea mix and coat.
4. The chickpea salad can be served chilled or at room temp.
5. Enjoy your healthy and delicious Chickpea Salad.

Classic Cucumber Salad

Serving Size: 4

Preparation Time: 10 minutes

Cooking Time: 0 minutes

Ingredients:

- 2 large cucumbers, thinly sliced
- 1/2 cup of thinly sliced red onion
- 1/4 cup of chopped fresh dill
- 1/4 cup of apple cider vinegar
- 1 tablespoon granulated sugar
- 1/2 teaspoon salt
- 1/4 teaspoon black pepper

Instructions:

1. Combine the chopped fresh dill, red onion, cucumbers and sliced red onion in a large bowl.
2. Mix together the apple cider vinegar and granulated sugar in a separate bowl. Stir until the sugar is dissolved.
3. Mix the vinegar and cucumber mixture together. Stir to combine.
4. Cover and keep in the refrigerator for at least 30 mins before you serve.

CHAPTER 7: DESSERT RECIPES

Strawberry Popsicles

Preparation time: 15 minutes

Cooking time: 5 minutes

Serving: 8-10 popsicles

Ingredients:

- 2 cups of fresh strawberries
- 1/4 cup of honey or granulated sugar
- 1/4 cup of water
- 1/4 cup of fresh lemon juice

Instructions:

1. Strawberries should be washed and hulled. Then, blend them in a blender until smooth.
2. Heat the honey or sugar in a small saucepan over medium heat, stirring occasionally.
3. Mix the sugar syrup with the lemon juice and stir.
4. Mix the sugar syrup and strawberry puree in a large bowl. Stir well.
5. Mix the ingredients in a mold and place them in a container.
6. The popsicles should be frozen for at least four hours or until they are completely frozen.
7. Serve by running the molds under warm water for several seconds to loosen the popsicles.

Baked Pears

Serving: This recipe makes 8 servings.

Preparation time: 10 minutes

Cooking time: 30-40 minutes.

Ingredients:

- 4 pears
- 2 tablespoons unsalted butter
- 1/4 cup of brown sugar
- 1/4 cup of chopped walnuts
- 1/4 teaspoon cinnamon
- 1/4 teaspoon nutmeg
- 1/2 cup of water

Instructions:

1. Preheat your oven to 375°F.
2. Pears should be cut in half lengthwise. The seeds and core should then be removed using a spoon.
3. Place the pear halves cut side up in a baking dish.
4. Mix together the brown sugar and walnuts with cinnamon in a small bowl.
5. Heat the butter in a small saucepan on low heat. Stir in the sugar and nuts mixture until well combined.
6. Spread the mixture on top of the pear halves.
7. Put the water in the bottom of the baking pan.
8. Bake the pears for between 30-40 minutes or until they become soft and tender.
9. Take the cake out of the oven and allow it to cool down for a while before serving.

Creamy Chocolate Pudding

Servings: 4 to 6

Preparation time: 15 minutes

Cooking time: 10 minutes

Chilling time: 2 hours

Ingredients

- 1/2 cup of granulated sugar
- 1/4 cup of cornstarch
- 1/4 cup of unsweetened cocoa powder
- 1/4 teaspoon salt
- 2 cups of whole milk
- 1/2 cup of heavy cream
- 4 ounces semisweet chocolate, chopped
- 2 teaspoons vanilla extract

Instructions

1. Mix the sugar, cornstarch and cocoa powder in a medium saucepan.
2. Slowly whisk in the heavy cream and milk until it is smooth.
3. Mix the ingredients over medium heat and continue to whisk until it comes to a simmer. It should thicken in about 8-10 minutes.
4. Reduced the heat to low and add the vanilla extract and chopped chocolate. Whisk until smooth.
5. Divide the pudding between 4 to 6 cups or other serving dishes.
6. To prevent any skin formation, cover each dish with plastic wrap and press the wrap directly onto its surface.
7. Allow the puddings to chill in the refrigerator for at most 2 hours or until they are set.

Frozen Berry Yogurt

Servings: 4 to 6

Preparation time: 5 minutes

Freezing time: 4 hours

Ingredients:

- 2 cups of frozen mixed berries
- 2 cups of plain Greek yogurt
- 1/2 cup of honey
- 1 tablespoon freshly squeezed lemon juice

Instructions:

1. Blend the Greek yogurt, frozen berries, honey, and lemon zest in a blender.
2. Make it creamy by blending.
3. Place the mixture in a container that is freezer-safe with a lid.
4. Cover the container with plastic wrap and freeze it for at least 4 hours or overnight.
5. Let the frozen yogurt cool in the refrigerator for about 10 to 15 minutes.
6. Serve the frozen yogurt immediately in a bowl or cone.

Made in United States
North Haven, CT
30 May 2023

37147737R00050